C000186397

Breaking Bounds
Six Newnham Lives

Breaking Bounds
Six Newnham Lives

EDITED BY

BIDDY PASSMORE

Published by
Newnham College
Cambridge CB3 9DF
www.newn.cam.ac.uk

© Compilation and introduction Newnham College,
individual essays the authors 2014

Apart from any fair dealing for the purposes of research or private study
or criticism or review, as permitted under the Copyright Designs and
Patents Act 1988, this publication may only be reproduced, stored or
transmitted, in any form or by any means, with the prior consent of the
publishers, or in the case of reprographic reproduction in accordance
with the terms of licences issued by the Copyright Licensing Agency.
Enquiries concerning reproduction outside those terms should be sent
to the publisher.

The moral rights of the authors in this publication have been asserted.

A CIP catalogue record for this book is available from the
British Library

ISBN 978-0-9930715-0-8

Design and layout Perilla Kinchin, White Cockade Publishing
Printed and bound by TJ International Ltd, Padstow

Front cover: *Majorie Blandy taking part in an operation, 1914 (detail of image on p.61). Courtesy of Imperial War Museum.*

Back cover: *Newnham College gardens.*

Frontispiece: *Students on the Mound in Newnham College gardens, 1919.*

Page 13: *Detail of the Clough Gates beneath the Pfeiffer Arch, the original entrance to the College, erected in memory of the first Principal, Anne Jemima Clough (1820–92).*

CONTENTS

THE CONTRIBUTORS

JENN ASHWORTH (b.1982, NC 2000) is a novelist and short
story writer. Born in Preston, Lancashire, and brought up as a
Mormon, she studied English at Newnham and creative writing
at the Centre for New Writing at the University of Manchester.
Her first novel, *A Kind of Intimacy* (2009), won a 2010 Betty
Trask Award. After the publication of her second, *Cold Light*,
in 2011, she featured on the BBC's Culture Show as one of
the UK's twelve best new novelists. Her third novel, *The Friday
Gospels*, about a Mormon family in Lancashire, was published in
2013. She has been a librarian in a men's prison and lectures in
creative writing at Lancaster University.

MARGARET DRABBLE (b.1939, NC 1957) is a novelist, biographer and critic. She has written eighteen novels (her first, *A
Summer Bird Cage*, was published in 1963; her third, *The Millstone*,
brought her the John Llewellyn Rhys Memorial Prize in 1966),
several screenplays, plays and short stories, and biographies of
Arnold Bennett and Angus Wilson. She edited two editions of
The Oxford Companion to English Literature, in 1985 and 2000. A
collection of her short stories, *A Day in the Life of a Smiling Woman*,
was published in 2011. She was made a Dame Commander of
the British Empire in 2008.

ELAINE FEINSTEIN (b.1930, NC 1949) is a poet, novelist,
playwright, biographer and translator. Her poems have been
widely anthologised and her versions of the poems of Marina
Tsvetaeva, for which she received three translation awards from
the Arts Council, were first published in 1971 and remain in
print. Her novels include *The Circle*, long-listed for the 'lost' Man
Booker prize in 2010. Her five biographies include studies of
Tsvetaeva, Pushkin and Ted Hughes and Anna Akhmatova,

(*Anna of all the Russias*, 2005). Her books have been translated into most European languages. Her memoir, *It Goes With the Territory: Memoirs of a Poet*, was published in 2013.

SARAH LEFANU (b.1953, NC 1971) is an author and broadcaster. Born in Aberdeen and brought up there and in East Africa, she was Senior Editor at the Women's Press in the 1980s and 1990s, responsible for their innovative science fiction list. Her first book was *In the Chinks of the World Machine: Feminism and Science Fiction* (1988). Other books include *Rose Macaulay* (2003), *Dreaming of Rose: A Biographer's Journal* (2013) and *S is for Samora: A Lexical Biography of Samora Machel and the Mozambican Dream* (2012). She read English at Newnham and teaches English Literature and Community Engagement at the University of Bristol.

SUE LIMB (b.1946, NC 1965) read English at Newnham. After graduating she researched Elizabethan poetry before teaching English in a school, a prison and as a private tutor. She is the co-author of a biography of Captain Oates, and has written many novels, including the Jess Jordan series for young adults. A broadcaster on programmes such as *Quote Unquote* and *The Write Stuff*, she has also written a number of comedy series for Radio 4, most recently *Gloomsbury*, about the Bloomsbury Group. As Dulcie Domum, she wrote 'Bad Housekeeping', a weekly column in the *Guardian*, from 1988 to 2001, coining the term 'bonkbuster' in 1989.

CLAIRE TOMALIN (b.1933, NC 1951) is an author and journalist, best known for her biographies of Mary Wollstonecraft (her first book, in 1974), Katharine Mansfield, Nelly Ternan (*The Invisible Woman*), Mrs Jordan, Jane Austen, Samuel Pepys, Thomas Hardy and Charles Dickens (2011). After reading English at Newnham, she worked in publishing and journalism, becoming literary editor of the *New Statesman*, then of *The Sunday Times*, while bringing up her children.

EDITOR'S PREFACE

The idea for this collection of biographical essays came to me during a meeting of the Newnham Roll Committee. We were discussing ways to mark the 100th anniversary of the Roll – the college's alumnae association – which falls in 2018. (Newnham plans ahead.)

How about a book? I thought. Newnham has produced so many wonderful writers – a fact not generally known. Surely some of them would like to write about remarkable but less well-known Newnhamites from the past? We could produce 'a good read', boost the image of the college and make some money for bursaries. And why wait till 2018? I got the committee's approval and started on what seemed a straightforward task

Of course, it wasn't quite as simple as that. Successful writers are busy people. They not only write: they lecture, they travel, they teach. Some wanted to contribute but could not spare the time; one or two said yes and then had to withdraw. But nearly all who replied liked the idea and wanted to do something for their old college. And the fact that this book has appeared despite setbacks is largely due to help cheerfully volunteered by alumnae.

First thanks go to my editorial advisers, both friends from Newnham days and both, as it happens, classicists who drifted: Susie Harries, prize-winning biographer of Pevsner, and Perilla Kinchin of White Cockade Publishing, who nobly – and in the midst of other work – took on design and layout. Special thanks also to my son Luke Ridley for constant technical assistance and wizardry with photographs.

At Newnham, Development Director Penny Hubbard, Catherine Seville, the Vice Principal (who chairs the Literary Archive Committee), and Jean Gooder, former Director of Studies in English, gave encouragement and good advice. Anne Thomson, College Archivist, spent hours – no, days – looking into possible biographical subjects, unearthing wonderful pictures and scanning them, often at short notice. But thanks must go above all to the six writers, who agreed to research and write a 2000-word biographical essay for no fee and bore it bravely when a mere modern linguist turned journalist dared to meddle with their prose. Special mention must be made of Claire Tomalin, who supported the project from the start, was the first to 'bag' her subject, and wrote an immaculate piece in record time despite many distractions.

Among those who provided pictures and information, I should like to single out Sigrid Pohl Perry of the special collections library at Northwestern University, for producing pictures of Constance Garnett with speed and efficiency, and Constance's great grandson Oliver, who gave by return permission to use them. Elaine Andrews of Morley College eagerly produced fine photographs and useful information about Amber Reeves. Clare Heath, new consultant to Camellia plc, which holds the Amy Levy archive, was happy to give access to the splendid image of Amy in her black hat. Others who gave help beyond the call of duty are thanked by individual writers in their source notes.

Biddy Passmore (NC 1970)

PICTURE CREDITS

Unless otherwise stated, all photographs come from the archives of Newnham College Cambridge and are reproduced with the kind permission of the Principal and Fellows.

Portraits facing the start of essays are extracted from group photographs taken while the subject was at Newnham. In most cases, the group portrait appears later in the essay; Majorie Blandy appears on p.42 together with Amber Reeves (both 1908). No picture is available of Enid Welsford as a student at Newnham: her portrait is extracted from a 1936 staff group.

p.18 Sergey Stepniak, p.20 Constance Garnett with David, p.24 Constance Garnett in old age: supplied by the Charles Deering McCormick Library of Special Collections, Northwestern University, Illinois, and used with the kind permission of Oliver Garnett

p.33 Amy Levy in London late 1880s: courtesy of Camellia plc

p.45 Amber Reeves Blanco White at the Lambeth exhibition, p.47 poster as Labour candidate, p.49 teaching in the 1950s: courtesy of Morley College

p.54 Majorie Blandy's 1914 passport, p.56 The Women's Hospital Corps outside Claridge's, p.59 Majorie doing the high jump: courtesy of her son, Christopher Martin

p.61 An operation in progress at Claridge's: Imperial War Museum

p.78 Peggy and her mother, p.80 Peggy at Cambridge, early 1920s: courtesy of her niece, Kitty Turnbull

p.83 Peggy Pollard in old age, p.84 Peggy on pilgrimage to Vierzehnheiligen, pp.86–7 walls of Peggy's bedsit in Truro: courtesy of Claire Riche

Introduction

DAME CAROL BLACK

Principal of Newnham College

It is hard to believe that I have already been Head of House at Newnham for two years. Time has flown by. I have found the experience fulfilling, challenging and exciting. Newnham has a proud history of educating women, undergraduates and graduates, and supporting female academics dating back to 1871 – and is still, uniquely, pursuing that mission today. Although I had no previous experience of single sex education – I was educated at a mixed grammar school and Bristol University – I have been able to build on my years of championing women's development and careers, particularly in the field of medicine and healthcare.

Newnham's students are bright, talented, articulate and active; the Senior Members and staff lively, committed, hard-working and friendly. An outstanding features of Newnham is the concern shown for students' welfare and well-being – the support given by Senior Members and staff and by students to each other. The College recognises that women's academic performance is enhanced by developing their self-confidence and resilience, and women here are encouraged to flourish and succeed.

Reading the six biographical sketches presented here will amply demonstrate this supportive atmosphere, apparent from the College's earliest years. The women featured, all but one born before 1900, were in rebellion to some degree against convention. They thirsted for the independence and self-fulfilment a good education would bring. They longed for the freedom to learn, to debate, and to hold their own in the company of other intelligent people. They also wanted to pass on their knowledge and ideas to help others, as they themselves had been helped: no fewer than four of them had attended schools founded by the very first students at Newnham. One of those four – Enid Welsford – stayed on to teach at the College, becoming the first Director of Studies in English and inspiring a whole generation of young women to become writers.

This is one of the main reasons for the astonishing number of distinguished writers that Newnham has produced. Most, but by no means all, read English; others have been historians, classicists, social and natural scientists … Six of the best have contributed to this volume, their chosen subjects ranging from a brilliant translator through feminist writers and a conservationist to a pioneering doctor. We are very grateful indeed for their time and support for this project.

This book, then, is Newnham on Newnham. It is also Newnham for the benefit of Newnham: proceeds from sales will go towards College bursary funds, to help support students across the entire range of subjects studied here.

I hope you enjoy reading it.

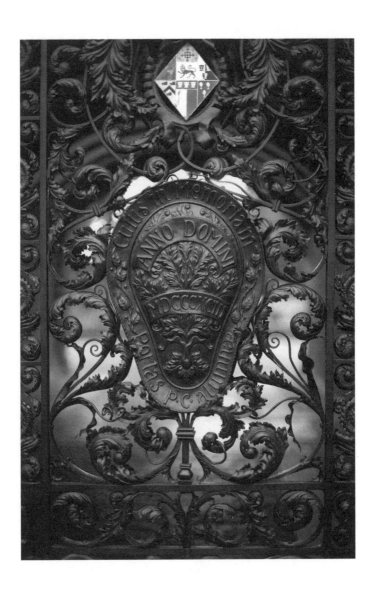

Constance Garnett
(1861–1946)

CLAIRE TOMALIN

Constance Garnett was one of Newnham's earliest students, and went on to a life of high thinking, plain living, hard work and outstanding achievement. The task she chose was to make Russian literature of the 19th century accessible to the English. Between 1894 and 1928, despite poor health and failing eyesight, she translated Tolstoy, Turgenev, Goncharov, Ostrovsky, Herzen and Gogol. She brought Chekhov to the English stage for the first time. She made the earliest English translation of Dostoevsky's *The Brothers Karamazov*, setting off a wave of enthusiasm for his work, and then took on the rest of his novels. Like all translators she has attracted criticism, but she is still admired by Russian and English scholars, and is read with pleasure to this day.

She was born Constance Clara Black in 1861, in Brighton, the sixth in a family of eight. Her childhood was difficult. At the age of three she was invalided for several years by an operation for a tubercular hip. She learnt to read early, and her clever, free-thinking mother and elder brothers and sisters taught her mathematics, science, geography, French and German. So from the start her imagination and intellectual curiosity travelled far and she was interested in

15

language. When she was twelve her father became paralysed
and a year later her mother died of the effects of trying
to lift him. Constance, overwhelmed with grief, found the
words to say what she felt: that to live without her mother
was like trying to live without air or bread.

Soon she rejected religion as her mother had done,
remaining an atheist thereafter. At the newly founded
Brighton High School for Girls she encountered Edith
Creak, a splendid headmistress fresh from Cambridge,
where she had been one of the first five students to
register in 1871 at the boarding house that developed into
Newnham College and had passed the Mathematical and
Classical Tripos. Under Miss Creak's guidance Constance
sat Cambridge Senior Local examinations for girls and
won the highest marks in England. She was offered a
scholarship of £35 a year for three years at Newnham,
now established on its site. The fees were £60 a year, and
her father agreed to pay the difference. In October 1879
she became one of the privileged students with a room in
the only building, then called Newnham Hall (now Old
Hall). 'The beauty of Cambridge was overwhelming,'
she wrote later, 'it made me feel too much moved. I was
constantly wanting to cry … I had never seen a beautiful
building before.'

She loved her room, in which the sofa had to be turned
into her bed at night, desk into dressing table, wash stand
screened off, and bath brought in. The food was terrible, ill
cooked, sometimes fermented. All lights were turned off at
10 pm. Constance could not afford good clothes or shoes.
But she was happy, and made friends, among them the
future mothers of Maynard Keynes and Frances Cornford.
The principal, Miss Clough, took an interest in every girl.
King's College welcomed Newnham girls to their lectures.

Constance Black, fourth from the right in the back row, in a photograph taken outside Newnham Hall (later Old Hall) at Newnham in 1880. The redoubtable principal Miss Clough is seated in the centre.

Constance excelled at Greek, both language and philosophy, and in June 1883 she was awarded a First.

A term teaching Classics at Newnham told her that she did not want to become an academic. Instead she went to London as a governess. Among her pupils were the children of Charles Booth, the social researcher, and she later contributed to his *Life and Labour of the People in London*, from her own observations of Whitechapel and the Mile End Road, where she became librarian at the People's Palace, newly built to bring culture to the East End poor. Social questions interested her, and she was horrified by the many prostitutes she saw in the West End. Her elder sister Clementina was established in London as a writer and lecturer on social and feminist issues, a friend of the Marx family and a Fabian, and Constance too joined the Fabian Society. There she was greatly admired by Bernard Shaw, who would have proposed marriage had he not felt he was too poor.

Her next admirer was a thin, clever boy of eighteen, Edward Garnett, son of the Keeper of Printed Books at the British Museum. He had left school at sixteen and seemed to be doing nothing: when Shaw asked her about the pretty boy, she said she was undertaking his education. Teaching led to love. Edward found work as a publisher's reader, they married in 1889 and rented a cottage in Surrey. Here they made friends with Felix Volkhovsky, a Russian political exile, and he suggested to Constance that she should learn Russian. Her enthusiasm led her to begin translating a story by Goncharov (author of *Oblomov*), as a way of learning. Meanwhile, in February 1892, her son David was born, an adored child who fully lived up to his parents' high expectations.

Another Russian exile came into their lives, a charismatic nihilist who went by the name of Stepniak ('man of the Steppes'). He encouraged Constance to take up translation professionally, and helped her with her studies. Her interest in Russian exiles was inspired by political sympathy, possibly

Sergey Stepniak, a studio portrait by Elliott & Fry, London.

encouraged by the fact that her grandfather had lived and died in St Petersburg, as naval architect to the Tsar Nicholas I, and both her father and uncle had grown up there. She fell in love with Stepniak. He was also married, and there was no affair, but the situation unsettled her and Edward.

Early in 1893 the Black family faced a brutal tragedy as the brilliant and gentle Arthur, the eldest sibling, murdered his wife and child and killed himself, without warning or explanation. Constance dealt with the horror by refusing to talk about it, and for the rest of her life she remained silent on the subject.

The following winter she travelled alone to Russia to improve her knowledge of the language and make literary contacts: a demonstration of her professional approach to the career she was embarking on, and of independence. David was left in the good care of his father and aunts. She took the train from Flushing to St Petersburg, where she met a friend of Chekhov and talked of translating his story 'Ward 6'. In Moscow she visited Tolstoy and was invited back. He wanted her to translate his book on the Gospels – she had already done a version of his *The Kingdom of God is Within You* – and she explained that her English publisher would not take on religious works. Tolstoy offered her *Resurrection*: sadly she never translated that late, great novel. She made tremendous trips in sledges through snowy forests, visited schools and peasant communities, and friends of Stepniak. Deep snow prevented her finding her grandfather's grave. By the end of the trip she could understand and speak Russian more easily, and she arrived home looking young and revitalised.

Now she was elected to the Executive Committee of the Fabians. She published her first Turgenev translations to acclaim. At the same time a volume of poems by Edward was badly reviewed, he was depressed and seemed close to a breakdown. Constance wrote him loving letters, and a collaboration on a shared project helped the situation: they

Constance with her son David, c.1894.

agreed they would build a house on Crockham Hill, near
Edenbridge in Kent. It was paid for with £1000 inherited
from her father, built of roughly cut local stone and wood,
and set in a meadow half a mile from any road. A well had
to be dug to sixty feet to supply water. There were open fires,
no electricity, and the privy was outside, but the view over
the Weald was incomparable. They named it The Cearne,
and Constance regarded it as home for the rest of her life.

Edward emerged from gloom and was becoming recognised as the most perceptive of readers in publishing. He was the first to see the greatness of Conrad and D. H. Lawrence, and encouraged Edward Thomas, Galsworthy and W. H. Hudson. Many of his authors were entertained at The Cearne by Constance. So the Garnett marriage was held together by shared literary interests and by their love of their child and their house. But they kept separate bedrooms. Edward was much in London, and in 1898 began a liaison with a young painter, Nellie Heath, which lasted to the end of his life. Constance accepted it and was fond of Nellie, but she wanted no scandal and the relationship was discreetly managed.

At Christmas 1899 Stepniak was killed as he crossed a railway line. His funeral was attended by William Morris, Eleanor Marx, Kropotkin, Keir Hardie and every Socialist, Anarchist and Nihilist who could get to London. Constance suffered 'unspeakable anguish' in silence. She was translating Turgenev and Ostrovsky, and now she began on *Anna Karenina*, then *The Death of Ivan Ilyich* and *War and Peace* – her publisher Heinemann paying her pro rata, 12 shillings per 1000 words.

Her eyes were so seriously weakened by this work that she had to give them a long rest. A second trip to Russia in 1904 was enlivened by taking David; the Russians were at war with Japan and disturbed by revolutionary plots. Tolstoy was in trouble and she could not visit him. On their return she took a flat in Hampstead so that David could go to day school. She saw friends – the Galsworthys especially – enjoyed theatre-going and joined in a Women's Suffrage procession. She translated *The Cherry Orchard* on spec in 1906 and sent it to the Stage Society, which made no initial response. She attended the Russian Social

Democrats' congress in Islington in 1907, met Trotsky, Lenin, who impressed her, and the future Stalin, who seemed to her a crook.

Arnold Bennett read *The Brothers Karamazov* in French, and urged her to translate it, and she, agreeing that it was a masterpiece, decided to go ahead. The problem with her eyes was dealt with partly by employing Russian-speaking women friends to read the text aloud and take dictation of her translation. (Mishearing may explain some of her slips.) In the midst of her labours, the Stage Society finally put on *The Cherry Orchard* at the Aldwych in May 1911. There were two performances, and although almost all the reviews were bad, a few saw the point.*

But Dostoevsky took the English by storm, and Constance was kept busy throughout the First World War with his works. At the same time she persuaded Chatto & Windus to commission translations of Chekhov's stories, working on them from 1916 to 1922, then the plays and the letters. Chekhov too became immensely popular, and Constance drew praise from critics and fellow writers. She greeted the news of the Russian revolution with rejoicing. The 1920s brought the death of her sister Clementina, but also David's marriage and two much loved grandsons; and his novel *Lady into Fox* brought him fame. Chekhov plays were produced more often, and from 1924 the BBC paid her royalties on their productions. She translated Gogol and Herzen's memoirs. She was earning enough to take winter holidays in France or Majorca to escape the cold, and in 1929 The Cearne acquired electricity. Her 71st and last volume, Turgenev's play *A Month in the Country*, appeared in 1934.

* John Palmer of *Saturday Review* found it the 'first great and original comedy produced since the beginning of my career', Frank Swinnerton was 'entranced, surrounded by empty seats', and Arnold Bennett liked it.

In 1926 she supported the workers in the English General Strike. She kept herself informed about Russia, and in 1933 she wrote to Leonard Woolf at the *New Statesman* in response to a review he had written of a book describing current conditions there. She explained:

> During the last forty years I have had many Russian friends, all sympathetic with the Revolution, many active revolutionaries. I rejoiced in 1917. Only very slowly and reluctantly, step by step, I have been driven by the desire to face the facts into my present position … after 16 years of Communist rule the disqualifications due to birth and education and the inequalities of rights (even down to the right to a food card) are far more oppressive than ever in the past (since 1861 anyway).

She gave as her conclusion, 'Communism is a fanatical religion. Is anything more to be dreaded by all lovers of free thought and culture?' Her letter seems to have been intended for publication, but it was – shamefully – not printed and survived only because one of her assistants kept a copy.

Edward died in London in 1937. In 1938 her translation of Chekhov's *Three Sisters* directed by Michel St Denis played for three months in London. During the Second World War she lived mostly on her own at The Cearne, wearing a helmet to do her gardening while the Battle of Britain was fought overhead. She stored apples and bottled fruit. She knitted her own clothes. The weak tea she drank became plain hot water. Her son and grandsons visited her and two granddaughters were born. Although she relished good conversation she liked to be alone. She listened to the radio. And when peace came she was invited to contribute her ideas about translation to the Third Programme.

This was in November 1946. Delighted to be asked, she prepared notes, giving them to David, to be used for the broadcast. But on 17 December she died, clear in her mind to the last, and with no fear of death. Had she lived two years longer, she could have been given her degree in Cambridge.

Constance Garnett in old age.

She was never part of the establishment, or even the Bloomsbury establishment into which her son married.* She did not care about honours, fame or money. She disliked organised religion but approved the Sermon on the Mount. She detested aristocracy and privilege, bureaucracy and government interference. She was an enthusiast, a socialist and revolutionary when young, deciding later that Marx's interpretation of history disregarded many of the most important motives for human actions. And she was a worker who changed the literary climate of England. She deserves to be better remembered and honoured.

Note on Sources

Carolyn Gold Heilbrun (1926–2003) was an American feminist academic who taught at Columbia and wrote many works of literary theory as well as detective stories. Her *The Garnett Family* (London: George Allen & Unwin, 1961) was a pioneering study that celebrated their selfless service to English letters through several generations and with no regard for fame or money – a trait Constance fully shared with them.

H. N. Brailsford (1873–1958), who knew CG personally, wrote the original Dictionary of National Biography entry (1924), naming her grandparents and summarising her life. Of her translations he wrote, 'This immense achievement was possible only because she worked rapidly, with unflagging concentration. Into it she put more than a scrupulous literary conscience and a scientific respect for both the languages in which she worked; she felt for the Russia of the last century a warm affection ... To innumerable readers she revealed a new world ...'

The longer, second Oxford DNB entry (2004) by the Russian scholar Patrick Waddington fills in details of her friendships with Russian exiles in England and the partial breakdown of her marriage. It also touches on her faults as a translator – stiff dialogue and errors, 'but she eschews linguistic fads or slang' – and Conrad's judgment is given, in which he compared her Turgenev translations to 'a great musician interpreting a great composer'.

In 1991 Richard Garnett, CG's elder grandson, published a biography of his grandmother, whom he knew well as a boy, *Constance Garnett: A Heroic Life* (London: Sinclair-Stevenson, 1991). Carefully and fully researched, it is entertainingly written and offers an admirable portrait.

---

* Vanessa Bell described her as 'not very exciting but very nice and full of valuable hints about fowls and vegetables'.

Amy Levy
(1861–1888)

JENN ASHWORTH

When Amy Levy was a child, living with her parents in what is now South Lambeth, she owned a 'Confessions Book' – a kind of quiz book pre-printed with questions about likes and dislikes, favourite writers, and so on – the stuff of parlour games and rainy-day amusements. From Amy's confessions book we discover that she liked 'green peas and lemonade', admired Bathsheba Everdene and enjoyed 'lazing on the grass with a good book or amusing friend'. One of the questions invited Amy to list what she considered to be the finest qualities in a man. The next, the finest qualities in a woman. Intriguingly, delightfully, young Amy answered the questions as one, refusing to assign a gender to virtues she believed belonged equally to both sexes. 'Good looks, good manners, intelligence, independence and a tendency to like me', she wrote. The confessions book also shows Amy's wit: for a writer who would come to be known for her 'minor' tone, her suicide examined in more detail than her work, she could be lively and amusing. She decided Satan's favourite poet was Aphra Behn and his favourite motto was 'take care of number one'.

Amy Levy lived at a turbulent time of great political and intellectual transition: she was born only two years after Jews were accorded full political rights in England, during the first flowering of feminism but a full seventy years before women were granted the right to claim their degrees at Cambridge, and during the period when the full impact of the work of Darwin, Marx and Freud started to be felt. She may have been a 'New Woman' – autonomous, financially independent, educated and unmarried – but her roots were traditional. She came from a large, loving family, comfortably middle class and modern in outlook. Homemade magazines that Amy wrote with her sisters (she was the second born of seven children) show an early interest in fiction writing and journalism, and a warm, humorous relationship with her siblings.

Her parents, Isabelle and Lewis, were Jewish but only casually observant of traditional dietary laws and committed to educating their daughters. Accordingly, Amy learned some Hebrew as a child and was later, aged fourteen, sent to the Brighton High School for Girls. There she became friends with Clementina Black, who would become a novelist and publicist, and her sister Constance (later Garnett), the future translator of Leo Tolstoy, Fyodor Dostoevsky and Anton Chekhov. The school's headmistress, Edith Creak, had been one of the first five women to attend what became Newnham College. During her time at school Amy grew to admire Edith's independence and education greatly, and versions of Edith began to appear in her early, unpublished, short fiction. Edith was perhaps the first financially independent and educated woman she had met; the fact that Creak was single was not lost on Amy, and would become important to her later.

In 1879, Amy followed in Edith's footsteps to Newnham and became the second Jewish woman to study at Cambridge* and the first at Newnham. She studied classical and modern languages and literature. Some of her writings – in particular her poems 'Alma Mater' and 'Cambridge' – suggest that she was unhappy there, or at least, dissatisfied with her creative output during this period. Linda Beckman Hunt reprints an unpublished poem in Amy's geology textbook entitled 'To Myself'. The work is painful in its self-castigation and demon-

Amy's headmistress, Edith Creak, top, as a student at Newnham, c.1874.

strates Amy's single-minded ambition: 'The brain is not first rate. YOU do great things? You strut as Poet? Pshaw!'

This self-deprecation seems incredible given that at just eighteen Amy was already a published poet and essayist. The feminist publication *The Pelican* had published one of her poems, 'The Ballad of Ida Grey', when she was only thirteen. From the age of seventeen

---

* The first was Hertha Ayrton, who entered Girton College in 1876 and became a distinguished physicist and the first female member of the Institution of Electrical Engineers.

she had been regularly publishing articles on culture, religious freedom and women's rights in the *Jewish Chronicle*. A closer reading of Amy's creative work at this time suggests that it was not the environment at Newnham that made her unhappy. Some of her biographers believe that in pursuing education and the life of a 'New Woman' she feared that at only twenty she was already unmarriageable. Several short stories written during this period show her wrestling with the paths open to her – on the one hand, marriage and motherhood, on the other, the intellectual life of the New Woman.

Lallie: A Cambridge Sketch expresses very clearly the pain and difficulty that could be caused by the transformative effect of women's education. The main character, a 'Newton girl', is described as 'a modern production, the offspring of a period of social and intellectual transition, and as such, was it to be wondered if she bore the marks of acute physical pain?' *Between Two Stools* (1883) re-examines this theme in a more comic tone, but shows Amy's continuing fascination with it.

The critical response to Amy's work has also bifurcated, many reading her as a 'New Woman' poet, while others concentrate on her Anglo-Jewish identity. Her best-known short story, *Cohen of Trinity*, focuses on a successful Jewish writer who publishes a work that is 'half poem' and 'half essay', realises he will never be accepted into English aristocratic society, and at the height of his literary success commits suicide; it suggests that Amy was well aware of the difficulties of both claiming and reconciling her marginal identities as a woman intellectual, English Jew and (perhaps) lesbian. The idea that she might need to sacrifice sexual love and companionship in order to secure the writing life she so wanted for herself seemed to distress

Amy Levy, fifth from the left in the back row of the group of students at Norwich House, overflow accommodation for Newnham, in 1880. She was the only one to sign her name with initials alone.

her greatly. This, along with some enduring problems with her health and hearing, may have triggered her recurring episodes of depression – an illness she suffered from throughout her teens and adult life.

Amy left Newnham after two years without taking the Tripos exams, even though in 1881 (the year she left) Cambridge women had won the right to sit them – a hard-fought-for triumph. Already her first collection of poems, a thirty-page volume entitled *Xantippe and Other*

Verse (1881), had been published. If Amy had stayed on at Newnham she might have had a more prescriptive course of study fixed on her. It is possible she felt independent study better suited her literary ambitions. Or she may have felt formal education had nothing more to teach her and life out in the world would prepare her best for the career she sought.

Whatever the reason, Amy spent four years travelling in Europe, particularly enjoying tracing the footsteps of Elizabeth Barrett Browning in Florence. Here she became friends with the essayist and writer Vernon Lee, a woman six years older, well connected in literary circles, and the subject of Amy's sonnet 'To Vernon Lee'. Many believe Amy had a physical affair with Vernon and indeed they exchanged passionate letters until Amy's death.

When Amy was not in Europe she was back in London, living with her parents and attending various debating and discussion groups. Like many New Women of her time, she was culturally and intellectually engaged with her peers, used to travelling around the city unchaperoned. Amy's freedom of movement was remarkable: this was Jack the Ripper's London, and women who moved freely about the city and beyond were often equated with prostitutes. She was keenly aware of this, as her poem 'Ballade of an Omnibus' ironically relates:

> Princess, your splendour you require,
> I, my simplicity; agree
> Neither to rate lower nor higher.
> An omnibus suffices me.

While in London, she met regularly with a group of women writers and radicals in the British Museum Reading Room, including Dollie Radford, Constance

Amy Levy, photographed by Alfred Goodman-Levy, Cumberland Place, London, probably in the late 1880s.

and Clementina Black, Olive Schreiner, Eleanor Marx, Beatrice Potter (later Webb) and her cousin Margaret Harkness. She also attended the meetings of the Fellowship of the New Life, the Social Democratic Federation, the Fabian Society, and a Men and Women's Club founded by Karl Pearson, a mathematician, prominent intellectual and socialist.

The period after Amy left Newnham was creatively fecund and her output was prodigious. In addition to composing two more poetry collections, *A Minor Poet and Other Verse* (1884) and *A London Plane Tree* (which was published posthumously in 1889), she wrote three novels, *The Romance of a Shop* (1888), about four sisters earning their living, *Reuben Sachs* (1888), and *Miss Meredith* (1889). True to her feminist convictions, she was determined to earn money: supporting herself financially had been a goal since she had met Edith Creak, and Amy always kept a detailed record of the payments that she received for her work.

Many of Amy Levy's contemporaries remarked upon her Jewishness, her habit of wearing comfortable, looser clothing and eschewing the corset (in common with many university-educated women of her time), and the sadness of her expression. Harry Quilter wrote after her death that 'I had rarely seen a face which was at once so interesting, so intellectual, so beautiful and alas! so unhappy [...] a small dark girl of unmistakably Jewish type, with eyes that seemed too large for the delicate features, and far too sad for their youthfulness'. She herself was intrigued (perhaps having internalised some of the anti-Semitism of her time) by the evocation and description of supposedly Jewish racial markers. She exaggerated this to the point of satire in *Reuben Sachs* and was misunderstood, receiving poor reviews that deeply upset her.

Reuben was in many ways a typical novel of its time – critical of the middle-class mores of Victorian society, the way marriages were brokered and contracted in the middle classes, and the stifling, dull lives that women were expected to lead. It was also a reaction to George Eliot's *Daniel Deronda*, which Amy felt romanticised the Jewish characters. It satirised both English and Anglo-Jewish society. As Julia Neuberger writes in her introduction to the 2001 Persephone edition of *Reuben Sachs*: 'This is a novel about women, and Jewish women, about public life, and Jewish public life, about families, and Jewish families, about snobbishness, and Jewish snobbishness.' As Amy deliberately focused on a Jewish family, and was unafraid to portray their particular vices and flaws, the novel was received critically within the Jewish community. However, modern readers have praised her satire, with Lisa Allardice describing Amy as 'a Jewish Jane Austen'.

It is likely that the disappointing reaction to *Reuben Sachs*, both within and without the Jewish community, as well as Amy's growing deafness, triggered her last bout of depression. On 10 September 1889 she lit some charcoal in the grate of her bedroom at her parents' house, where she had fled five days before, and sealed the room. She died in her sleep. Her friends, familiar with her history of depression, immediately recognised this as suicide. In the immediate aftermath of her death, gossip reigned as to the cause. Some believed she had been betrayed by her friend Karl Pearson, with whom she may have fallen in love: he had both excluded her from the meetings of the Men and Women's Club (which debated relations between the sexes) and unexpectedly announced his engagement to her intimate friend Olive Schreiner. Other contemporaries

Alma Mater

A haunted town thou art to me. – Andrew Lang

To-day in Florence all the air
Is soft with spring, with sunlight fair;
In the tall street gay folks are met;
Duomo and Tower gleam overhead,
Like jewels in the city set,
Fair-hued and many-faceted.
Against the old grey stones are piled
February violets, pale and sweet,
Whose scent of earth in woodland wild
Is wafted up and down the street.
The city's heart is glad; my own
Sits lightly on its bosom's throne.

Why is it that I see to-day,
Imaged as clear as in a dream,
A little city far away,
A churlish sky, a sluggish stream,
Tall clust'ring trees and gardens fair,
Dark birds that circle in the air,
Grey towers and fanes; on either hand,
Stretches of wind-swept meadow-land?
Oh, who can sound the human breast?
And this strange truth must be confessed;
That city do I love the best
Wherein my heart was heaviest!

Amy Levy's poem Alma Mater, *remembering Cambridge: published in* A London Plane-Tree and Other Verse *in 1889, the year of her suicide.*

speculated that the traditional, constricted life they thought her parents expected of her was the real cause of her unhappiness. Some speculated that it was Olive – not Karl – whom Amy had loved, and thinly veiled articles in the *Pall Mall Gazette* implied that the pair had indeed concocted a suicide pact that Olive had reneged upon.

A pioneer in life, Amy Levy also achieved another sad first in her death when she became the first Jewish woman in the country to be cremated. Oscar Wilde, writing just after Amy's death in the magazine he edited and to which she was a regular contributor, *Women's World*, used her obituary not to speculate about her personal life but to lavish praise on her work: 'To write thus at six-and-twenty is given to very few [...] The world must forgo the full fruition of her power.'

In 1890 the novelist and critic Grant Allen published an essay, 'The Girl of the Future', which examined 'the woman question' and named Amy Levy and other women like her as victims of the cultural move towards feminism and the education of women. 'A few hundred pallid little Amy Levys sacrificed on the way are as nothing before the face of our fashionable juggernaut. Newnham has slain its thousands and Girton its tens of thousands.' Rather than examining the constricting social context, the individual circumstances of her life, and her struggle with depression, some commentators turned Amy into an object lesson in the consequences of over-reaching. As a woman, a Jew, a lover of women and a writer with socialist leanings, she belonged to many groups about which society held stereotypes. For a while, the uniqueness of her perspective and the quality of her work were all but overshadowed by speculation about her death.

Yet she was a poet to the last, correcting the proofs of *A London Plane-Tree* just days before she died. And some of her posthumous publications, in particular *A Ballad of Religion and Marriage*, which was privately printed in an edition of twelve copies after her death, and which Christine Pullen considers Amy's 'literary suicide note', are among her most accomplished:

> Grant, in a million years at most,
> Folk shall be neither pairs nor odd —
> Alas! we sha'n't be there to boast
> 'Marriage has gone the way of God!'

For many years after its first publication in 1915, the *Ballad* was shelved in the 'Suppressed Safe' of the British Museum Reading Room – the place where works that were too controversial to be stored with the general catalogue were placed. A Ballad of Religion and Marriage almost reads as a prescient riposte to Grant Allen's assertions about the dangers of education for women and, indeed, one of the twelve copies of the print run was found among his papers after his death. In it, Amy Levy seems to come to the bleak conclusion that marriage, like religion, might save human society from chaos and anarchy, but within it, women are inevitably confined and powerless.

Note on Sources

Linda Hunt Beckman, *Amy Levy: Her Life and Letters*, Athens, Ohio: Ohio University Press, 2000

Alex Goody, 'Murder in Mile End: Amy Levy, Jewishness and the City', in *Victorian Literature and Culture*, Vol.34.2, 2006, pp.461-79

Iveta Jusova, *The New Woman and the Empire*, Columbus, Ohio: Ohio State University Press, 2005

Sally Ledger, *The New Woman: Fiction and Feminism at the Fin de Siècle*, Manchester: Manchester University Press, 1997

Julia Neuberger, in her preface to *Reuben Sachs*, London: Persephone Books, 2001

Christine Pullen, *The Woman Who Dared: A Biography of Amy Levy*, Kingston upon Thames: Kingston University Press, 2010

Edward Wagenknecht, *Daughters of the Covenant: Portraits of Six Jewish Women*, Amherst, Mass.: University of Massachusetts Press, 1983

Amber Reeves
(1887–1981)

MARGARET DRABBLE

Nearly ten years ago, when researching an introduction to the 2005 Penguin Classic edition of H .G. Wells's *Ann Veronica*, I first became intrigued by the life and work of Amber Reeves. I knew that she was the young woman on whom the engaging character of 21-year-old Veronica Stanley was based, and that she gave birth to Wells's daughter in December 1909 when she herself was 21, and newly graduated. I also knew that she had become Mrs Blanco White, a figure who was pointed out to me on several occasions in my Hampstead days, when she lived nearby in Downshire Hill. I never met her, but she was well known in the neighbourhood. She died in 1981 aged 94. However, by then she had more or less slipped out of literary history, and few were aware that she had herself become a writer of note. This neglect was, at the beginning of this century, on the way to being remedied. Her name appeared for the first time in the new edition of the Oxford Dictionary of National Biography, together with an article on her mother, the New Zealand-born Maud Pember Reeves (1865–1953), Fabian author of the classic sociological survey of poverty in Lambeth, *Round About a Pound a Week* (1913).

*Amber Reeves, second from right in the front row in the Newnham College
photograph of 1908. (Majorie Blandy's tall figure is fifth from the right
in the back row.)*

Amber was born in New Zealand in 1887, the oldest
of three children; her brother, Fabian, was to die in the
First World War at the age of 21. The family travelled
to England in 1897. Amber was educated at Kensington
High School, and in 1905 began her studies at Newnham
College, reading Moral Sciences, in which she achieved

a Double First in 1907 and 1908 (Part 2 in 'Metaphysical and Ethical Philosophy, together with the History of Modern Philosophy'). She said that she 'adored' her time at Cambridge, and she was highly regarded by her tutors, who included the economist John Neville Keynes, father of Maynard Keynes, who taught her logic, and described her as a 'clear and vigorous thinker'. Lively, beautiful, with (in the words of H.G. Wells) 'a sharp, bright, Levantine face under a shock of very fine abundant black hair, a slender, nimble body very much alive, and a quick greedy mind', she was nicknamed Dusa, after Medusa, a name that survives in the family. Her Newnham contemporaries included Katherine (Ka) Cox and Eva Spielman (later Eva Hubback), and she took an active part in college and university affairs and politics. More problematically, she also became involved at this time in a passionate love affair with H. G. Wells. It was this relationship, and the subsequent scandal, that eclipsed for a century her literary achievements and her work in education.

Wells was a friend of her parents, and a somewhat truculent member of the Fabian Society, which proceeded too slowly for his liking. The affair with Amber began when she was a promising member of the 'Fabian Nursery', and went to stay with H. G. and Jane Wells at their hospitable home in Sandgate, near Folkstone. Maud Pember Reeves wrote appreciatively to Jane Wells: 'You are good fairies to all these young people. It must be very pleasant to realise what a lot of happiness you give them.' But the seaside romance soon turned into something more turbulent and troubling, which became the focus of a great deal of gossip, gossip which intensified when Wells published *Ann Veronica*, with its all too easily recognisable heroine.

It was Amber Reeves's misfortune that so many in her parents' circle were well known writers and diarists, whose accounts as hostile witnesses have been preserved. (Bernard Shaw was to call her 'an ungovernable young devil' in a letter to H. G. Wells in August 1909.) Beatrice Webb was particularly outraged by the notion that Amber had been seduced 'within the very walls of Newnham, [Wells] having been permitted, as an old friend, to go to her room.' Webb's diary comments and letters on the subject are sharp. She described her (15 September 1908) as:

> the brilliant Amber Reeves, the double first Moral Science Tripos, an amazingly vital person and I suppose very clever, but a terrible little pagan – vain, egotistical, and careless of other people's happiness ... however, the little person can work, and work and play at the same time. A somewhat dangerous friendship is springing up between her and H. G. Wells. I think they are both too soundly self-interested to do more than cause poor Jane Wells some fearful feelings, but if Amber were my child I should be anxious.

The anxiety would have been well founded. When Amber found she was pregnant, she and Wells briefly eloped to Le Touquet, but were unhappy there, and Amber was persuaded to marry a young lawyer, Rivers Blanco White (with whom she was to bear two more children). She took refuge in a country cottage discovered for her by the feminist actor and novelist Elizabeth Robins, author of the influential play *Votes for Women* (1907). Here, in secrecy, clouded by scandal, sheltered by a chivalric marriage of convenience, her intellectual trajectory might have been halted. Amber Blanco White might have retreated into domesticity and dwindled into a wife.

But she did not. She did not take to housework, and never liked to cook. Instead, she made for herself a career as a writer, lecturer and activist. During the First World War, she worked at the Admiralty, and later as Director of Women's Wages at the Ministry of Munitions. She published at least eight books, some under her maiden name, some under her married name, including volumes on propaganda, economics and the nationalisation of banking. At the adult education institution, Morley College in South London, where her Newnham friend, Eva Hubback, was Principal, she lectured on philosophy and psychology from

Amber Reeves in one of her distinctive hats minding the Morley College stand at the Lambeth Exhibition in 1948.

1928; she became acting head for a year when Eva died in 1949 and continued as tutor until 1965.

Amber Reeves also published four novels. The first, *The Reward of Virtue* (1911), is about the inadequacies of conventional female education, and dwells particularly effectively on its naive heroine's ignorance about money, and her habit, when she found herself not very happily married, of going shopping and running up large bills because she had nothing better to do – a sequence which foreshadows a similar theme of female extravagance in Wells's *Marriage* (1912). This reminds us that Amber's mother Maud and her father William were said to have quarrelled a great deal about money: Maud had been shocked to discover that upon marriage her husband had expected to take charge of her finances, and, when she inherited money later in life, she avoided handing her bequests over to him. Women, she warned, should not be financially dependent upon men. The daughter was to inherit her mother's social concerns.

Money also provided the dominant theme of Reeves's second and best novel, *A Lady and her Husband* (1914), written when she had three small children to care for. This deals even more trenchantly with domestic finance, patriarchal authority, and with the nature of capitalism itself. It too is a form of *Bildungsroman*, in which the heroine discovers her own inadequacies and learns from them; but the protagonist here is a conventional good-hearted 46-year-old married woman, Mary Heyham, who finds herself at a loose end when her three children grow up and leave the nest. Under pressure from her youngest, free-thinking socialist 18-year-old daughter Rosemary, she decides to educate herself about the nature of her husband's thriving catering business: she examines the hard lives of his waitress-employees (just as

*As Mrs A. Blanco White, Amber Reeves stood unsucessfully for Parliament
as a Labour candidate in 1931.*

Amber's mother had scrutinised the lives and finances of the mothers of Lambeth) and decides to take up their cause. When her husband plans to turn his business into a public company, she realises he cannot do this without her consent as a major shareholder, for he has invested heavily in her name. She works out that the employees will fare even worse at the hands of a public company, run for the benefit of dividends and shareholders, and stubbornly refuses, to his wrath, to sign away her rights.

The most curious and interesting section of the novel comes towards the end, when Mary leaves home secretly in order to think things through. Realising that 'she had lived like an insect in a coral reef, ignorant of the laws by which it was governed', she resolves to enlarge her understanding. With a sense that her 'intellectual life was only beginning', she takes a flat in Chelsea, where, for a week, she battles with such works as *The Shareholder's Guide to Company Law*. And she is very happy alone in her flat, where nobody can find her. Far from being frightened by the unaccustomed solitude, she rejoices in it. The flat is decorated in bright, Bohemian colours, which glow in the text: a Japanese orange and red sofa, a bedroom of Chinese blue, sea-green and indigo. She is happy in her freedom and in 'the gay reassurance of the beautiful room'.

The ending returns to the conventional: she does not concede, for she has discovered that her financial and legal position is impregnable, but she goes back to her husband when he agrees that he would be better advised to change tack and go in for philanthropy and politics. On her return to her large London town house, she reflects that 'the entrance hall was more like a dream … in its tall ugliness, than the queer red and orange room that they had left to the windy night'. She settles back into her life of ease and

Amber Reeves Blanco White teaching a psychology class at Morley College in the 1950s.

servants, but with a new confidence, a new sense of expectation and engagement.

Reeves's other novels, *Helen in Love* (1916) and *Give and Take: A Novel of Intrigue* (1923) are less successful, but the dissident spirit of *A Lady and her Husband* continues to glow like a prophetic beacon. It is a very early treatment of the theme of a woman's need for a room of her own. (Woolf's lectures and essay on the subject came more than a decade later: they too had a Newnham connection.) Mary Heyham's pleasure in her runaway solitude (and her husband's desire to keep the truth of her disappearance from the servants) finds a haunting real-life echo in a memorial of Mrs Yates Thompson, the respectable, enormously wealthy, shy and philanthropic daughter of George Smith, publisher of Charlotte Bronte and of the original

Dictionary of National Biography. Thompson was one day seized by 'a desire to taste this wild fruit, liberty', and, when her husband was away for a few days, she evaded the butler, made off with her toothbrush and nightgown, and took a train to somewhere 'utterly unknown to her, put up at a modest hotel, and came home the next day. The butler as he let her in betrayed no sign.' She remembered her escapade with pleasure, indicating the hotel to a companion a few months before her death in 1941 with the words 'This is the place where I stayed the night once. And no one ever knew.'

This anecdote is told by Reeves's friend and defender Elizabeth Robins in a sketch, *Portrait of a Lady* (1941), first published by the Hogarth Press and reprinted at Newnham in 2002. Newnham's first library, built in 1897 and extended in 1907, was endowed by Mr and Mrs Yates Thompson. There are connections, there is continuity.

Forty years later, Doris Lessing addressed the subject of the secret room, in one of her darkest and most influential stories, *To Room Nineteen*. Here a seemingly happily married woman with four children becomes increasingly depressed, rents a room in a seedy hotel, where she sits day after day doing nothing, in a 'dark creative trance', until she commits suicide. This was published in 1963, in a collection called *A Man and Two Women*. This was the year when Sylvia Plath committed suicide.

Amber Reeves Blanco White, as we have seen, survived her appointment with death in Room Nineteen, and lived a full, long and active life. A woman's room, she once wrote, was 'her adventure, her defence, her stronghold'. She was a pioneer, and a survivor.

Note on Sources

This essay is adapted and expanded from an article first published in the *Guardian* in 2005, which drew on Sally Alexander's entries on Amber Reeves and Maud Pember Reeves in the 2004 edition of the Oxford Dictionary of National Biography.

Other sources include:

R. Fry, *Maud and Amber: A New Zealand Mother and Daughter and the Women's Cause, 1865–1981*, Christchurch, NZ: Canterbury University Press, 1992

M. Holroyd, *Bernard Shaw: The One-Volume Definitive Edition*, London: Vintage, 1998

N. MacKenzie and J. MacKenzie, eds, *The Diary of Beatrice Webb*, 4 vols, London: Virago, 1982-5

G. P. Wells, ed., *H. G. Wells in Love*, London: Faber & Faber, 1984

Elizabeth Robins, *Portrait of a Lady, or the English Spirit Old and New*, London: Hogarth Press, 1941; reprinted privately by Newnham College, 2002, to commemorate the building of the new library, with an afterword by Jean Gooder

Majorie Blandy
(1887–1937)

SARAH LEFANU

The passport is dated 24 September 1914. In cursive typescript as flowery as the phrases, Sir Edward Grey, His Majesty's Principal Secretary of State for Foreign Affairs, requests and requires 'all those whom it may concern to allow Miss Majorie Ada Blandy, British subject, travelling to France, to pass freely without let or hindrance and to afford her every assistance and protection of which she may stand in need.'

It gives her age as 27, and her profession as Physician & Surgeon. The photograph shows clear eyes, a wide brow, a generous mouth and smooth, glossy hair. It is a beautiful face with more than a hint of determination. A slip of paper glued to the official form bears her signature: Majorie A Blandy.

Majorie* was on her way to Paris, one of a handful of English women doctors who took part in the massive mobilisation of medical services on the Western Front in the First World War. In this, as throughout her life, she was a pioneer, a feminist who shunned the barricades but quietly pushed the boundaries of what women could achieve.

---

* A spelling she used all her life but pronounced 'Marjorie', as far as we know. She was always 'Minkie' or 'Minx' within the family.

Majorie Blandy's passport, issued 24 September 1914.

Freshly qualified to practise, she was off to use her skills in the war effort in the only way open to her: by joining the Women's Hospital Corps (WHC), newly set up by Doctors Flora Murray and Louisa (daughter of the redoubtable Elizabeth) Garrett Anderson.

Unlike Dr Elsie Inglis from Edinburgh, who had approached the War Office offering to supply qualified women doctors and been told to 'go home and sit still', Drs Murray and Garrett Anderson hadn't wasted their time with the British authorities. As militant suffragists – they were both members of the Women's Social and Political Union – they'd had dealings with the Home Office and gained an insight into the 'cherished prejudices and stereotyped outlook of officials', in Flora Murray's words. They knew that to approach the War Office would only mean a rebuff. Even the British Red Cross turned them away, despite the reputation of its Chief Commissioner, Sir Arthur Sloggett, as 'a great man with the ladies'. ('I expect we are not his kind of ladies', remarked Flora Murray.) But through the French embassy they approached the French Red Cross, offered their services and were accepted. Elsie Inglis too would find a berth for her Scottish Women's Hospital Unit with the French Red Cross.

On 14 September the Women's Hospital Corps – five doctors and a handful of orderlies – had arrived in Paris and moved into the newly-built and rather grand Hôtel Claridge on the Champs-Elysées, which had been commandeered as a hospital for Allied soldiers. It would become Hôpital Auxiliaire 137, or, more familiarly, 'Claridge's'. With the arrival on 27 September of Majorie and her friend Rosalie Jobson, also newly-qualified, the number of doctors rose to seven.

The seven doctors of the Women's Hospital Corps, with two senior orderlies, outside Claridge's. In the back row between the two new arrivals (Majorie Blandy on the left, Rosalie Jobson on the right) is another Newnham graduate, Grace Judge, a few years older. Flora Murray is in the front row, far right, next to Louisa Garrett Anderson. On the verandah lies one of the patients in his hospital bed. Taken in September 1914. (Courtesy Christopher Martin)

For the patients, wrote Flora Murray:

> Women doctors were a novelty which served to enhance the importance and the grandeur of the gilded and marble halls in which they found themselves. 'The doctors is ladies,' they wrote in their letters home; and to the visitor who asked: 'Is it really true that you have no men doctors here?' the reply was: 'And what will we be wanting men doctors for, sir?'

Majorie Blandy soon settled in. Less radical than the WHC's leaders (she was a member of two non-militant suffragist groups, the International Woman Suffrage Alliance and the London Society for Women's Suffrage) she had, like them, a determination to succeed as a professional woman and a warm human sympathy with the wounded men.

She was from an unusual background. Born on the island of Gran Canaria in 1887, she was the fifth of six children of a younger son of the wine-making Blandy dynasty of Madeira. Could the odd spelling of her name have been a mistake by a Spanish-speaking clerk who registered her birth at the British Consulate? We do not know. Her passport and a few photographs are rare documents in a life otherwise largely undocumented. She left no written record – no journals, diaries, personal letters nor even postcards have survived. And she was born too long ago for a biographer to draw on living memories, except those of her surviving son Christopher, who was still a child when she died.

While we know tantalisingly little about her inner life, we do know something of her family background and of the world she grew up to inhabit. By September 1914, when the passport was issued, her life had taken her from the Canary Isles via London to Jersey, where her father, a difficult and quixotic man, set himself up for a few years in the port wine business; on to Newnham College Cambridge in 1905 to study natural sciences; and then in 1909 to the London School of Medicine for Women, the first medical school in England where women could train.

Her resolve to pursue a proper education – and, perhaps, to succeed in a man's world – seems to have come during her teenage years in Jersey, when she came under the influence of Newnham through her headmistress. The brisk and lively Elsie Roberts, Principal of the Jersey Ladies' College which Majorie attended from fourteen to eighteen, had herself been at Newnham as an 'out' student in 1879–80. It was probably at her urging that the clever schoolgirl applied to study there and chose science.

This was a challenging proposition for a woman at Cambridge in 1905. Eight subjects made up the Natural Sciences Tripos – chemistry, physics, mineralogy, geology, botany, zoology and comparative anatomy, human anatomy and physiology – and most of them were not taught at Newnham but at men's colleges, to which women had to be chaperoned. (The Master of Trinity demanded a promise from Miss Clough, Principal of Newnham, that her students would never enter his college unchaperoned.) But some were taught at Newnham. One-legged Miss Freund – she had lost a leg in a cycling accident – with her strong Austrian accent ('Have I got you wiz me in zat?') ran the chemistry lab, now the Old Labs, in the gardens. Outside the lab the College pony, wearing little leather boots to protect the grass, pulled the lawnmower. Miss Freund was a bit of a joker. She would send her students to revise the Periodic Table, and they would find it laid out in the lab with the divisions marked in Edinburgh Rock, and the elements made of little cakes with names and atomic weights picked out in icing.

According to her son Christopher, Majorie threw herself into college life. As well as amateur theatricals and cocoa parties, debating was all the rage. The three Halls competed vigorously in debates on free will and predestination, the place of women, the relativity of morals, and whether or not each Hall should have its own cat. But she excelled above all at sport. A strong swimmer, she also became a star hockey player, for which female students wore navy blue

serge skirts ending twelve inches above the ground, so shockingly short that no man was ever allowed near the field where games were played. Majorie played hockey against Oxford and thus would have been a Blue had women been granted such sporting honours.

Majorie jumping 4ft 6in. at Newnham.

Not all women students sat Tripos examinations. Cambridge University, after all, did not grant degrees to women; astonishingly, it would not do so for another forty years. But they were 'allowed' to take the examinations and in 1908 Majorie Blandy took her Part I papers and passed.

That summer she left Newnham and returned to Jersey. Her mother had recently died of appendicitis and with her father's departure for Dominica on yet another harebrained scheme (a timber venture this time, which ate up the remains of his fortune), there was little to keep her there. (The youngest child, Richard Dennis, six years her junior, was still at boarding school.) Majorie had to decide on her future. Her father's erratic career and frequent financial difficulties must have increased the attractions of a solid professional training that would give her financial independence. Perhaps she had long cherished dreams of becoming a doctor. Now, with the intellectual confidence and scientific knowledge acquired at Newnham, she knew she could make a go of it and she enrolled the following autumn at the London School of Medicine for Women, based at the Royal Free Hospital.

In September 1914, at Claridge's, Majorie was finally starting out on the career she had chosen. But she didn't stay long in Paris. Within a few weeks, she and two others were sent north to Boulogne, on loan, as it were, to the doctors of the Royal Army Medical Corps (RAMC). During that first autumn of the Great War, the RAMC, housed in makeshift hospitals on the north coast of France, was struggling to cope with the influx of sick and wounded men pouring in from Ypres and other battlefields along the bitterly contested lines of the Western Front.

No. 13 Stationary Hospital, Boulogne, where Majorie was posted, offered a different level of experience altogether from Claridge's, and that had been shock enough for a young woman straight from medical school. It boasted no gilded and marble halls. It offered only crowded wards, corridors crammed with wounded men on stretchers, a constant struggle against the ubiquitous and tenacious lice and the all-pervasive, mousy stink of gas-gangrene.

On 29 October nurse Kate Finzi, also at 13 Stationary, wrote that she and her colleagues simply had no time to think of their own feelings. 'Fingerless hands, lungs pierced, arms and legs pretty well gangrenous, others already threatening tetanus (against which they are now beginning to inoculate patients), mouths swollen beyond all recognition with bullet shots, fractured femurs, shattered jaws, sightless eyes, ugly scalp wounds; yet never a murmur, never a groan except in sleep,' she wrote. By December

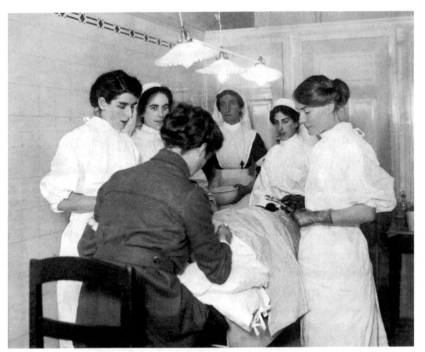

An operation in progress at Claridge's. Majorie Blandy stands on the right, holding a pair of bonecutters, as Flora Murray, her back to the camera, delivers the anaesthetic. Published in the Daily Sketch, 17 October 1914. (Courtesy IWM)

they were seeing cases of frostbite, some of them so severe they had to be amputated below the knee.

Claridge's, meanwhile, had become too expensive and difficult to heat and it closed on 18 January 1915. The Women's Hospital Corps moved north, and set up a hospital just outside Boulogne, at Wimereux, under the auspices once more of the French Red Cross, but now with official recognition from the War Office and the RAMC. Majorie joined them there. But by March that year the armies were digging themselves into their trenches for the long haul, and hospital treatment was moved back to Britain. Back in London, with the support – alone amongst the top brass – of Sir Alfred Keogh, Director General in Britain of the Army Medical Services, Flora Murray and Louisa Garrett Anderson set up the Endell Street Military Hospital. This was staffed entirely by women.

Majorie did not go with them. Instead, ambitious to upgrade her qualifications from the English Conjoint Diploma to a full medical degree, she went back to the Royal Free where she worked as house surgeon and physician while studying for her MB and BS (Lond). With those under her belt she moved, in February 1917, to the Hospital for Sick Children (later the Great Ormond Street Hospital for Sick Children). She was joined there by Rosalie Jobson until, with the return of male doctors from war work the following year, all women doctors were dismissed; the hospital would not employ women again as doctors for another twenty years. The senior physician under whom Majorie was working, Arthur Francis Voelcker, ended the testimonial he wrote for her with the words: 'Her work has been quietly, thoroughly, loyally and intelligently done throughout her appointment the termination of which I much regret.'

Majorie applied for a job as junior house physician at the National Hospital for the Relief and Cure of the Paralysed and Epileptic (later the National Hospital for Nervous Diseases) in Queen Square, where no such discrimination was in place. She boldly demanded a salary of £200 a year, which was twice what she had been earning at the Hospital for Sick Children. Someone must have realised how good she was. In October 1920 she was appointed their first female Medical Registrar. She continued to gather qualifications, passing the difficult and demanding Membership exam for the Royal College of Physicians in 1922.

She was now thirty-five and still single. Had she perhaps lost a lover, as had so many other women, in the Great War? Had she deliberately chosen, over marriage and motherhood, the interests and satisfactions that a career as a doctor offered? Or had it been marriage itself – her mother's experience painfully in mind – that she had deliberately avoided? Perhaps, more simply, the right man had not yet turned up.

That year, however, an Irishman called James Purdon Martin (Binje to his family), arrived from the Royal Southern Hospital in Liverpool to take up a post as house physician, a position somewhat junior to Majorie's. He was six years younger than her, a few inches taller, slim, long-legged and attractive. They were married on 15 September 1922 at St Pancras registry office.

Majorie stayed on at Queen Square, later taking on a simultaneous subsidiary post as assistant physician at the Elizabeth Garrett Anderson Hospital (EGA). Many if not most institutions required women to resign as soon as they married, but not the National Hospital. Majorie continued working there until she was six months pregnant. Unremarkable now perhaps, but in those days extremely unusual.

A son, Christopher, was born in July 1924, and a second son, Gavin, three years later. The family moved from a flat near Euston to a house in Golders Green and then to another overlooking Hampstead Heath. Majorie continued working at the EGA. She also worked as a Medical Officer at baby and child clinics in Islington and Hampstead, and at another hospital run by women, the Bermondsey Medical Mission Hospital in south London.

The crowded pavements of London along which she tramped from one place of work to another were very different from the bleached and wind-scoured beaches on which she'd run free when she was a young child and growing girl. Before her marriage, she had frequently visited friends near Kimmeridge Bay on the Dorset coast, and had fallen in love with the wide sweep of its fossil-rich, mudstone cliffs. Now she took her sons there for summer holidays. Christopher recalls long, happy weeks with their adored mother, turf beneath their feet and seabirds soaring overhead.

The boys' childhood idyll was not to last. Majorie was Senior Physician at the EGA when, in 1933 or 1934, she first noticed the symptoms of breast cancer. She kept it secret from her family. Visits to the Marie Curie Hospital for Women (founded in 1929 by Newnham graduate Helen Chambers) went unremarked. 'She was always in and out of hospitals,' Christopher remembers, 'so we didn't think anything of it.' In September 1937 she took thirteen-year-old Christopher to settle him at his new school, Gresham's, in Norfolk. It was the last trip she made. She died in October, aged only fifty.

Her obituary in *The Lancet* read:

In her professional work Dr Blandy was, as in everything else, unusual. Her knowledge was orthodox, but her approach to her cases was individual, unconventional, and with an immense regard for the human factor. Her bedside manner was her natural manner, sparing of words almost to bluntness, humorous, shrewd, infinitely kind. As a diagnostician she was outstanding, and she put her gift most generously at the disposal of her colleagues.

Sources and Acknowledgments

E. K. Bradfield, G. F. Gabb, H. Wilson, in Ann Phillips, ed., *A Newnham Anthology*, Cambridge: Newnham, 1979

Eileen Crofton, *The Women of Royaumont: A Scottish Women's Hospital on the Western Front*, East Linton: Tuckwell Press, 1997

Susan Cohen, *Medical Services in the First World War*, Oxford: Shire Publications, 2014

Kate Finzi, in Anne Powell, ed., *Women in the War Zone: Hospital Service in the First World War,* Stroud: History Press, 2009

Lyn Macdonald, *The Roses of No Man's Land*, London: Michael Joseph, 1980; Penguin edition 2013

Flora Murray, *Women as Army Surgeons*, London: Hodder & Stoughton, 1920

Archives:

Newnham College
Great Ormond Street Hospital for Sick Children
National Hospital for Nervous Diseases

Thanks to:

Nicholas Baldwin (GOSH), Dick Blandy, Jackie Cheshire (National Hospital), Dr Christopher Collins, Dr Jennian Geddes, Jean Gooder (Newnham), Christopher Martin, Maggie Martin, Katrina Mayson, and Anne Thomson (Newnham)

Enid Welsford
(1892–1981)

ELAINE FEINSTEIN

Enid Welsford shared the quality she ascribed to Chaplin in her scholarly masterpiece *The Fool*: a gift for self-mockery without any loss of self-esteem. She liked to tell stories against herself. It gave her an extraordinary spiritual resilience. For all her habitual cheerfulness, Enid Welsford was well aware that the facts of human life are tragic. She lost her much loved younger brother in the Great War and the pain remained: she dedicated her first book *The Court Masque* to him in 1927. Her mother's death in 1935 was another loss she felt keenly. Her good humour came from finding a way of life she thoroughly enjoyed: teaching the literature she loved, alongside that 'long and delightful initiation into research' for which she thanked Professor H. M. Chadwick. And she always had a warm and affectionate circle of friends.

Enid was 57, and in her last years as Director of Studies in English at Newnham College, when she interviewed me as a candidate for admission in 1948. She was sitting in her room in Clough Hall on a floral loose-covered armchair with both legs tucked underneath her. Her demeanour was cheerful and her features girlish as she questioned me, and it was only when she stood up to escort me to the door that I saw for the first time that she was tiny.

Her height was part of her legend, rather like her relationship to the car she drove so boldly. It was said that she
was too short to see over the steering wheel, and that she
had to peer through it so that it looked as if the car was
driving itself. Those who were driven by her, some on a
generous trip to the Wool Churches of East Anglia, recall
the terrifying way she drove along Suffolk country lanes
without allowing for possible oncoming traffic.

Elsie Duncan-Jones, the distinguished scholar, writing
a tribute to Enid in *Cambridge Women: 12 Portraits* gives
us several accounts of her absent-mindedness. While
Pernel Strachey was Principal of Newnham, for
instance, she once returned an unmarked set of keys to
Enid, who received them gratefully and enquired how
Miss Strachey had known they belonged to her. Miss
Strachey put it down to elementary psychology. Among
other stories told by Elsie Duncan-Jones I like best the
tale of Enid being locked out of College in an evening
dress, failing to climb a wall, and having to crouch,
holding onto railings then outside the Kennedy building,
until rescued, giving rise to talk of a ghost in Sidgwick
Avenue.

Was there some connection between Enid's analysis of
the many incarnations of *The Fool* – sometimes monstrous,
often bullied, always felt, even when privileged, as an
anomalous figure – and her awareness of her own diminu-
tive stature? Elsie Duncan-Jones tells us that Enid had to
have all her clothes and shoes made specially for her, but
that she was nimble, even athletic, and enjoyed skiing,
skating and, for a time, fencing; all of which suggests a
complete refusal to be embarrassed by her size. Most of
her students over the years would confirm my memory of
Enid's sunny good humour.

 Enid's childhood seems to have been a happy one. Her father had been a Fellow of Gonville and Caius for seven years before becoming a mathematics teacher at Harrow School. Her mother, Mildred Laura Hancock, was a talented painter. The Alpine watercolours in Enid's room in Clough Hall were painted by her, and Enid must have felt a very close attachment to her mother, since she asked for her own ashes to be buried in the same grave.

Enid was a precocious child and her parents encouraged her passion for literature. When she was twelve, they had a book of her poems, *The Seagulls and Other Poems*, published privately and placed in the Cambridge University Library. Whether or not she continued to write poems in later life, she never lost her love for poetry.

Until 1909, the year her father died, she was educated at the Conamur School in Sandgate, Kent, a high-class boarding school, two of whose founding Principals, the Misses Pennycuick, had been at Newnham. At 17, Enid left home to study literature at University College, London, under W. P. Ker and took her first degree there in 1911. In the same year she went up to Newnham College, Cambridge, and in 1914 gained marks good enough for a First Class degree in the Medieval and Modern Languages Tripos, with a distinction in Old English. (English only became a full Tripos in its own right in 1929.) A Marion Kennedy studentship made it possible for her to study comparative literature under Professor H. M. Chadwick, a noted authority on Anglo-Saxon and Old Norse literature, thus opening the wide range of research which always fascinated her.

She was made an Associate Research Fellow at Newnham in 1918 and remained at the College for the rest of her life, elected to a Fellowship in 1921, and serving as the first Director of Studies in English, once the Tripos

Enid Welsford, standing on the left of the middle row in a group portrait of the Principal, Dame Myra Curtis, and Fellows of Newnham in 1950. The photograph was taken by Ramsey & Muspratt of Cambridge: the co-founder of the studio, Lettice Ramsey, was a Newnhamite.

was established, from 1929–52. Her range of responsibilities increased later. She served as Director of Studies in Archaeology and Anthropology from 1939 to 1952, and in Moral Sciences from 1941 to 1952.

Both the English Faculty and the University, by no means readily welcoming to women in the twenties and thirties, recognised her as an outstanding scholar. She was a lecturer in the Faculty of English from 1923, and University Lecturer from 1928 to 1959. In 1919 she also founded, with M. D. Haviland, the University Women's Research Club – dubbed The Informal Club – held in her College room, where students, liberally provided with sweets and cigarettes, could discuss the literary issues of the day. She established lifelong friendships with other scholars such as Elsie Duncan-Jones, Sita Narasimhan and Dorothea Krook.

The closest friendship of her life was made with the gifted and strikingly beautiful Nora Kershaw, whom she first met when they were both undergraduates at Newnham. They shared an interest in Anglo-Saxon literature, and for a time set up house together in Owlstone Road, though Nora was drawn away from Cambridge to take up a lectureship at St Andrews for some years. When a small inheritance made it possible for Nora to give up University teaching and devote herself entirely to research, she returned to Cambridge and began to do so with immense energy. She went on to marry Professor Chadwick, and although he was twenty years older than she was, they enjoyed a very happy partnership. Their house became a centre for those who shared the same literary enthusiasms. Nora may have seemed gentle, but she had a formidable intelligence and – as Enid notes – was able both to collaborate with her husband, and compel him to publish his research as an important book.

For a time, Enid became part of the Chadwick household and was always much influenced by their passion for Anglo-Saxon literature. Duncan-Jones recalls companionable morning coffees with Enid and Nora at Matthew's café in the centre of Cambridge, where there was laughter and good fellowship.

Enid had no great interest in current literary fashions. In 1928, when the University appointed her as a Lecturer, I. A. Richards, with his close analysis of texts, attracted far larger audiences than Enid. In my own undergraduate days I remember both A. P. Rossiter and F. R. Leavis exerting a similar pull. Enid's lectures and enthusiasms were far more traditional though indeed equally original. In those days, in any case, we were not encouraged to attend lectures, which consumed valuable reading time.

It was as a supervisor and a teacher of small groups of undergraduates that Enid was most influential and certainly that is how I remember her most vividly. Sita Narasimhan, who went on to become Director of Studies in English after Enid retired from that post, was astonished to find that once Enid discovered Sita's passionate interest in Marx and Gandhi, she made a point of reading both in depth, even going on to include the works of Lenin.

She was never dogmatic, always available to under-graduates with problems and effortlessly in command of any material she taught. We took particular pains with the essays we brought to her each week, and she always scrutinised them closely, paying particular attention to their structure and clarity. In seminars, she encouraged us to speak out freely. She could be stern, however. Claire Tomalin mentions failing to prepare Marlowe for a seminar, and being asked, 'Are you not interested in Marlowe, Claire?' She admits feeling deeply ashamed. Enid clearly liked Claire, nevertheless. On another occasion, she drove her through Suffolk to see the Wool Churches: 'We went into Clare, Long Melford, Lavenham, the Waldingfields and many other beautiful churches, the first time I had seen them. It was an extraordinarily kind thing to do.'

Claire felt close enough to invite Miss Welsford to her wedding in the Round Church in Cambridge and recalls that she pronounced Nick Tomalin 'the handsomest bride-groom she had ever seen'.

Antonia Byatt also remembers her with affection. 'The thing I remember most vividly about Miss Welsford is her offering us minute glasses of sherry and saying, "I think it is prudent to make oneself a promise never to drink before 6.00 p.m." – I think of her every day when I pour my 6 o'clock glass of champagne.'

ENID WELSFORD

Enid Welsford in 1968, a portrait taken by B. Gaye, Cambridge.

In 1968 Sue Limb, the writer and broadcaster, spent a summer in the big rambling house at 7 Grange Road which Enid then shared with Sita Narasimhan. She remembers Enid telling her that in her younger days, she had been invited to attend a meeting of the Apostles, and how terrified she had been of Wittgenstein.

Wittgenstein was among the most illustrious figures living in Cambridge in my first undergraduate years, known to have a very rigorous approach to all his students, though perhaps by then already ill. Certainly, he had not dealt kindly with two of Newnham's brightest undergraduates who came to him for supervision, and I remember Miss Welsford's indignation as she spoke of the unhappiness he had caused them. She thought a teacher so destructive of students' confidence was close to wicked.

In my third year, she supervised me for the Moral Sciences paper, though we sometimes discussed issues relating more properly to Tragedy. I remember vividly a conversation we had about Andromache yielding up her child to be murdered rather than sleep with the son of Achilles. I found the decision both indefensible and frankly implausible and said so. I may have been trying to test Miss Welsford's moral stance on sexual behaviour, though indeed I knew she was no prig. She objected strongly to Milton, in *Comus*, identifying goodness with power rather than love, and evil with sensuality rather than cruelty.

Miss Welsford reminded me that the Greeks had murdered Andromache's husband, Hector, and most of her family. Would I have allowed the commandant of Auschwitz to make love to me? She had a characteristic way of making a point, which often ended with an upturned, questioning: 'Do you ...?' as if checking that her listeners had followed her reasoning. I don't remember what I mumbled in reply. Nothing was off-limits for discussion with Miss Welsford, not even the tenets of her deeply held Christian beliefs.

She was always honoured as a scholar. She received a prize from the British Academy for *The Court Masque* (1927) and *The Fool* was widely acclaimed outside specialist journals, notably in the *Times Literary Supplement* and the *New York Times*. Jean Gooder, a later Director of Studies in English at Newnham, told me recently that it was Enid Welsford's *The Fool* which made her want to read English at the College, struck by a theme which ran from 'ancient myth and theatre, through medieval drama, Commedia del Arte and Shakespeare to the silent films of Charlie Chaplin' and offered 'nothing less than the cultural history of Europe and America'.

After Enid's retirement from teaching she continued her research, publishing a rather surprising paper on 'Salisbury Plain, a study in the development of Wordsworth's mind and art' in 1966, and *Fowre Hymnes, Epithalamion. A Study of Edmund Spenser's Doctrine of Love* in 1967. It is a source of some regret to me that I had returned to Cambridge by then, but felt too diffident to visit her.

Enid taught most of the women who read English at Newnham, and many who went on to make their own contributions to the literary world readily acknowledge her influence. As Margaret Drabble remarked (when I asked about her mother, who was also taught by Miss Welsford): 'I like to think of Enid's teaching "flowing down the generations".' Indeed, so it did.

Note on Sources

Elsie Duncan-Jones, 'Enid Welsford', in E. Shils and C. Blacker, eds, *Cambridge Women: 12 Portraits*, Cambridge: CUP, 1996

Enid Welsford, *In Memoriam: Nora K. Chadwick 1891–1972*, Cambridge: Newnham, 1973

Enid Welsford, *The Fool : his Social and Literary History*, London: Faber & Faber, 1935

Emails exchanged in 2014 with Antonia Byatt, Margaret Drabble, Jean Gooder, Sue Limb and Claire Tomalin

And memory, of course ...

Peggy Pollard
(1904–1996)

SUE LIMB

Peggy Pollard stares boldly out from the Newnham
Year Group photo of 1925, looking a bit like a sailor
with her short cropped hair and roll-neck sweater. She
was already a Sanskrit scholar, poet, musician and mystic,
but despite the severe expression she had a playful nature.
Peggy loved disguise, practical jokes and clandestine
projects, parodies, forgeries and slang.

Perhaps this was a reaction to her strict and conventional
upbringing. She was born Margaret Steuart Gladstone,
in London in March 1904, into the brilliant and power-
ful establishment family which had produced the Prime
Minister William Ewart Gladstone (who had died only six
years before Peggy's birth). Her father was a wealthy East
India merchant but also, alas, a textbook Victorian patriarch
who did not believe in educating women.

The establishment in Surrey where Peggy grew up had
ninety-nine acres and enjoyed the services of nine servants.
Dinner was always a full dress affair with parlour maids
in attendance. But these comforts came with a price:
conformity. One evening when the teenage Peggy dared
to come down to dinner without wearing her corset her
father threw a massive tantrum. How would she ever find

Peggy and her mother on the beach.

a wealthy husband with such a 'sloppy' figure?

Her mother was also a source of pressure and anxiety for Peggy, who described the maternal side of the family – the Irish Fitzgibbons – as discontented and ambitious. Peggy felt she failed to live up to her mother's expectations – a mother who, to exercise her frustrated intellect, set herself the task of learning a new language every year. Peggy suffered migraines for decades until her mother died in the 1960s, a liberation acknowledged by Peggy herself.

But Peggy enjoyed a different kind of full-blooded liberation much earlier. Her father died when she was sixteen, and in due course, after teaching herself Sanskrit and being interviewed by Miss Clough, she went up to Newnham in the autumn of 1922. She wanted to study Sanskrit because she had fallen under the spell of the god Vishnu: Peggy was given to sudden spiritual enthusiasms. At school she had identified a certain tree as sacred and worshipped it. In the course of her long life, religion became more and more central to her, though without any sacrifice of more earthly high spirits and frivolity.

When she arrived at Newnham, she plunged with gusto into a life free of stockings, gloves, corsets and all the paraphernalia of etiquette which had so imprisoned her mother. Dressing in a determinedly masculine style, she

was one night mistaken for a man and challenged by the
prowling Proctor, who, realising his mistake, doffed his
mortar board and fled. During what must have been quite
torrid Newnham tea-times and midnights, Peggy dabbled
once or twice in Sapphic love (strictly from the waist up)
but was equally interested in what must have been her
rather intimidated men friends.

She found that a few hours' study every morning in
Newnham library was more than enough for her purposes
– getting a First in Oriental Languages (she was the first
woman to do so). The rest of the day was often given over
to japes: forgeries, parodies and disguises. On one occasion
she and a friend dressed up as a grandmother and mother
and walked a faux baby around Cambridge in a pram.

Everyone had to have an alias, for Peggy loved playing
with language, often talked and wrote in Mockney, and
referred to women as 'Judies'. Despite, or perhaps because
of, her same-sex adventures Peggy was diverted to receive
almost simultaneous proposals of marriage from wealthy
and congenial Arthur Elton and a Cornishman, Frank
Pollard (Peggy nicknamed him Old Uncle Gregory at
Cambridge and, in later life, he was universally known as
Cap'n Pollard).

Elton and Pollard were both notorious woman-haters:
Elton because he preferred men, Pollard because he
preferred boats. Though Peggy was engaged for a while
to Elton, it was Pollard, penniless and without prospects,
whom she married in 1928.

Peggy seems to have approached her marriage, and
indeed all the major projects of her life, in a spirit of dare-
devil and carefree improvisation. She and Pollard agreed
there must be no children, and insisted that all references
to procreation be omitted from the marriage service, which

was concluded in a little over ten minutes. And when, on their honeymoon in St Ives, Pollard the sailor made it clear he was much more interested in canoeing than canoodling, Peggy came to terms swiftly with the fact that she had contracted a *mariage blanc*, and concluded that, as she and Pollard otherwise got on famously, and becoming a married woman had doubled her private income, all would be well. Not that Peggy was mercenary: quite the opposite. The moment she gained access to her fortune she started to give it away.

A certain lack of confidence in her physical appeal was bound to haunt her for a while, however. In fact she was tall and handsome, with a fine nose and piercing blue eyes. Her long earlobes she attributed in later life to heavy earrings, quipping that she always thought her earlobes would make a pleasant hors d'oeuvre for a cannibal.

Soon after their marriage, she and Pollard moved, lock stock and piano, down to St Mawes, where after a few years she was reassured about her personal charms by a prolonged and passionate affair with a woman violinist, and a one-night stand with a male pianist. Despite the

Peggy photographed while she was at Cambridge in the early 1920s.

prevailing bohemianism it is unlikely they ever performed as a trio.

However, having experienced human passion, Peggy seems to have turned her back on Eros and given herself over to Agape – compassionate love of humankind and adoration of the divine. She and Pollard settled in Truro and became famous locally, he for his work in local politics, she for her spiritual zeal.

So far Peggy's young life may seem like the flamboyant adventures of a rebel without a cause, but a cause soon presented itself. First of all, there was Cornwall – Pollard's home country, and of course, the most remote and exotic part of England, with its own language and culture. Peggy, always intrigued by the alien and esoteric, enthusiastically espoused all things Cornish, learning the language, becoming a bard of the Cornish Gorsedd, playing the harp and writing plays and poems. Her new identity as a Cornish bard enabled Peggy to acquire another alias: her bardic name was Arlodhes Ywerdhon, the Irish Lady. She also wrote *Cornwall*, a book of quirky and captivating insights about the county.

'When you cross the border from Devon,' she wrote, '…you should feel a foreigner. But you may one day become Cornish by adoption and grace. (I have heard that this can be achieved by falling out of a boat at St Mawes.)' Peggy certainly became Cornish by adoption and grace, but whether she received that maritime baptism is uncertain.

However, her major project in the 1930s had a national significance. Ruskin and later Trevelyan had warned of the industrialisation and urbanisation of the landscape. In 1928 Peggy formed 'Ferguson's Gang' inspired by Clough Williams-Ellis's book *England and the Octopus*, describing the dangers of ribbon development and the encroachments of suburbia. Clough later said that he would have dedicated the book to Peggy, had he been aware of her existence at the time.

Ferguson's Gang rescued historic buildings and important sites by collecting donations to buy the properties for the National Trust. They were essentially Peggy's friends. None of them was called Ferguson – that was another example of Peggy's addiction to smoke and mirrors. Of course, every member of the Gang had an alias. Peggy's was Bill Stickers, as in 'Bill Stickers will be Prosecuted', and the minutes of their meetings were written in what they called 'The Boo' because there was not room on the cover for the final 'k'. They often arrived for the meetings in fancy dress, followed by a Fortnum's van.

The opening entry in the 'Boo' is revealing: 'First Resolution: England is Stonehenge not Whitehall. Second Resolution: LUNCH'. They often used Mockney in their communications. 'I 'ave always preferred to be enonymous, and I done wot I could while I could', Peggy (or perhaps Bill Stickers) observed.

When they made their donations, or appeared at functions, it was always masked and in disguise in order to remain 'enonymous' – but of course, the charade of it all was great publicity for their cause. Over a decade they rescued seventeen properties and sites. They had a special interest in 'quintessential village architecture' and committed themselves to repairing and renovating buildings using traditional techniques.

By 1935 Peggy was also working with the Council for the Protection of Rural England to save the Cornish coastline, threatened by bungalows and caravan parks. She purchased several coves and clifftops with her own money and donated them to the National Trust – whilst always remaining 'enonymous'.

Peggy Pollard in old age, wearing her characteristic peasant-style dress.

Peggy's identity had always revolved around her faith, or faiths: with an enthusiasm embracing Russian Orthodox, Celtic and Vedic divinity, she had a truly ecumenical soul. However, she was an enthusiastic participant in the material world too. During the war, when Cap'n Pollard was away commanding minesweepers, she kept a flock of goats at the remote hamlet of Quenchwell, near Truro. Unsurprisingly, she bestowed on her goats the names of Vedic goddesses. And in the early 1950s she at last found time to complete her PhD: 'The Indian experience of Vishnu from the Rigveda down to the Puranas'.

Peggy on her first pilgrimage to Vierzehnheiligen in Bavaria in 1984, with the tapestry banner she had embroidered herself depicting the fourteen holy helpers to whom the basilica is dedicated. After her death in 1996, her ashes were laid to rest there at the 10th station of the cross.

For several years she served as an assistant to the evangelical Bishop of Truro, Dr J. W. Hunkin. Curiously, he was the Proctor who, decades earlier, had challenged her during her moonlit ramblings in Cambridge.

In middle age her mysticism deepened, and after Hunkin's death in 1950, Peggy converted to Roman Catholicism, which perhaps offered her poetic and ceremonious soul ampler opportunity for expression. She translated Old Church Slavonic Marian hymns, she stitched tapestries, vestments

and Catholic banners, she raised funds to sink wells for
some African nuns she had befriended, and she helped to
build a new Catholic Church in Truro.

On her eightieth birthday she led a pilgrimage to
the Basilica of Vierzehnheiligen in Bavaria. Peggy was
so enraptured by the place she called it her 'Heaven
on Earth' and asked that, after her death, her ashes
should be taken there. She also revelled in the enormous
German ice cream sundaes, spending a day interspers-
ing 'piety with gluttony'. (Thirteen years later, when her
friends returned to Vierzehnheiligen with Peggy's ashes,
they felt their duty was not completely discharged until
they had consumed a Peggy Pollard memorial ice cream
sundae.)

In her vigorous old age she was a familiar figure striding
around Truro. As her friend Claire Riche recalls:

> Peggy … had been a beauty in her youth and this still
> showed. She wore no make-up but her eyes, a clear blue,
> were both piercing and kindly. She was tall and slim.
> Her waist-length dark hair hung loosely in a net. Around
> her head she wore a scarf, tied peasant fashion, and over
> her long flowing black skirt a beige hessian apron. Both
> were heavily embroidered. She looked to all intents and
> purposes like a Russian peasant.

Peggy was fluent in Russian amongst other languages
and even taught it in a local school. And when, one
humdrum afternoon, the Blessed Virgin Mary suddenly
appeared to Peggy at home, sitting in an armchair, it
was in Russian that the supernatural visitor addressed
her, complaining that her shrine in Liskeard had fallen
out of use, and asking Peggy to reinstate it. Peggy later
discovered there had indeed been a shrine in Liskeard,

Two walls in Peggy's bedsit in Truro, where she lived into old age.

in a clearing between two pieces of woodland known as Ladye Park. The Shrine was restored and re-dedicated and became once more a place of pilgrimage.

If this event seems incredible, with Peggy Pollard nothing, however far-fetched, seems impossible. She had a taste for the bizarre and mysterious as well as a devout faith and a deep social conscience. She was fascinated by everything and had enormous intellectual vigour well into her nineties, after she had become bedridden and blind. She found riches in the odd and peripheral, but also in the overlooked simple things. The ending of her book about Cornwall could speak for her approach to life:

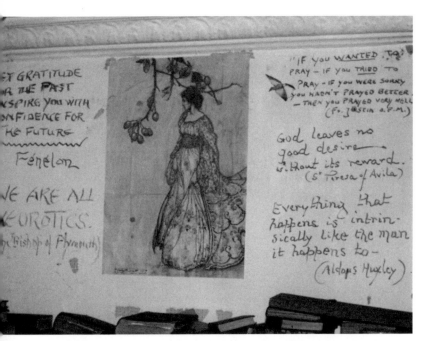

I have taken an edge-of-the-eye view of Cornwall, leaving out most of the important stuff and snipping bits off the more obscure sides of the subject. You can read about the important bits anywhere … but it is really things like the smell of escallonia that matter.

And if you ever stand on Pendannack Cliffs at Mullion, or gaze upon Lansallos Bay near Fowey, or pause on a certain footpath to admire the weirdly shaped offshore rock called the Irish Lady near Land's End, remember Peggy who saved them for us. Despite her disguises, aliases and eccentricities, despite the impression, sometimes, that her whole life was a rebellion against conformity or a picaresque spiritual odyssey, she left a lasting legacy.

Sources and Acknowledgements

Peggy Pollard, *Cornwall*, London: Paul Elek, 1947

Anna Hutton-North, *Ferguson's Gang, The Maidens Behind the Masks*, Lulu Inc., 2013

Claire Riche, *The Lost Shrine of Liskeard*, London: Saint Austin Press, 2002

Thanks to:

Kitty Turnbull, Peggy's niece, for reminiscences, and Polly Bagnall, whose book on Ferguson's Gang is in preparation at the time of writing